D0593241

Pine Forge Elementary
Boyertown Area Schools

Also by Robert Kraske

America the Beautiful: Stories of Patriotic Songs
Harry Houdini: Master of Magic
Is There Life in Outer Space?
Silent Sentinels: The Story of Locks, Vaults, and Burglar
    Alarms
The Statue of Liberty Comes to America
The Story of the Dictionary
The Treason of Benedict Arnold, 1780: An American Gen-
    eral Becomes His Country's First Traitor
Crystals of Life: The Story of Salt
The Sea Robbers

The TWELVE MILLION DOLLAR NOTE

Robert Kraske

Strange but True Tales of Messages Found in Seagoing Bottles

THOMAS NELSON INC., PUBLISHERS
Nashville   New York

Pine Forge Elementary
Boyertown Area Schools

For Bev and Ed Teague

Copyright © 1977 by Robert Kraske

All rights reserved under International and Pan-American Conventions. Published in Nashville, Tennessee, by Thomas Nelson Inc., Publishers, and simultaneously in Don Mills, Ontario, by Thomas Nelson & Sons (Canada) Limited. Manufactured in the United States of America.

First edition

Library of Congress Cataloging in Publication Data

Kraske, Robert.
    The twelve million dollar note.

    SUMMARY: A collection of true stories about notes found in bottles that were put into the ocean.
    1. Ocean bottles—Juvenile literature. 2. Drift bottles—Juvenile literature. [1. Ocean bottles. 2. Drift bottles] I. Title.
G532.K72   001.55   77–24164
ISBN 0–8407–6575–4

8799

Contents

1 • The Richest Boy in the Azores Islands . . . 9
   A Variety of Useful Services 15
2 • True Tales of Messages Found in
   Seagoing Bottles 19
   The Twelve Million Dollar Note 21
   The Blank Check in the Jam Jar 25
   The Ship That Turned Turtle 27
   Torpedoed Off Gibraltar 31
   The Man Who Received His Own Death
      Note Through the Mail 33
   A Pure Bowshot at 700 Meters 35
   Letter from a Dead Soldier 38
   Bottles That Came Home 39
   "Your Old Pal, Bill. . . " 42

Bottle Postmen That Deliver Letters
    from Lonely Hearts 43
Bottle Preachers Cast the Gospel
    Upon the Waters 50
Queen Elizabeth's Official Uncorker of
    Ocean Bottles! 53
The Bottle Message That Called Out
    the French Navy 57
Two Cats on a Ghost Ship 60
"Five Ponies, 150 Dogs Remaining . . ." ... 63
Cape Sheridan, 1905: Peary Was Here! 65

3 ● Charting Ocean Currents with
Seagoing Bottles   69
The First Oceanographers 73
Great Ocean Rivers 76
The Ends of the Earth 78
Much Useful Information 81
Private Groups 85
Recovery 88
Letters from the Finders 91

Index 95

Alone, alone, all, all alone,
Alone on a wide wide sea!

—*SAMUEL TAYLOR COLERIDGE*

·1·

The Richest Boy in the Azores Islands

The Azores are a group of nine islands in the Atlantic Ocean, about one thousand miles west of Portugal and about two thousand miles east of New York. The southeasternmost island is Santa Maria. Columbus stopped there in 1493 on his return trip from the New World to Spain. High among the vineyards in Santa Maria's green hills stands a chapel where the brave explorer gave thanks for his safe voyage.

One day a few years ago a twelve-year-old boy was walking along a narrow beach on Santa Maria looking for seashells that he could sell for a few pennies to the tourists who come to Vila do Porto, the island's only town. The boy was barefoot, and a rope tied around his waist held up ragged trousers. Over his shoulder hung a limp flour sack. It was empty today because the restless sea had cast little of value on the beach.

And then he almost stepped on it, a bottle nearly buried in wet sand. What was a bottle worth? A few pennies perhaps from a junk dealer. He pulled the bottle out of the sand. The next wave washed over the hole and left it filled with sand.

The boy's eyes narrowed. There was something unusual about this bottle. Both the cork and neck were covered with a thick coat of red wax. Inside he could see a roll of paper. On the paper was writing in some foreign language which he could not read. It was in English.

In Vila do Porto, he took the bottle to the priest.

"What have we here?" the old man said, his eyes twinkling. "I know! A treasure map cast ashore in a drifting bottle!"

The priest wrapped the bottle in a towel. He held the neck and tapped the bottle with a hammer. From the pieces of broken glass, he carefully lifted out the paper. He slipped on eyeglasses, winked at the boy, and began to read.

As he read, a frown came across his face. Then he took off his glasses and looked at the boy.

"Miguel, do you have any idea what this letter says? It says the finder of this bottle will get a reward of one thousand American dollars if only he will write a letter and say where he found the bottle."

He put on his glasses again and peered at the letter.

"He must write to this place in New York City, which"—he pointed through the open window at the sea and sky— "is to the west across the sea in America."

Miguel's dark eyes opened wide. "One thousand American dollars! That is more money than my father earns in a year, maybe two years, as a fisherman!"

The old priest looked down at the wood floor and bit his lip.

"My boy—Miguel—perhaps I should warn you." His voice grew soft. "Sometimes letters like this are a hoax—a joke, a trick. Sometimes people enjoy playing cruel jokes. It is possible, just possible, that this letter is a hoax."

Miguel's face fell. "Then I won't get a thousand dollars?"

"I don't know. Let's try writing to the address in America. We will give your name and tell where you found the bottle. Then we'll see. But" —he placed a gentle hand on the boy's shoulder— "perhaps you should prepare yourself for disappointment. It is very possible the money will not come."

Four weeks later, however, a letter from New York City came to the priest. Inside were a check for one thousand dollars with Miguel's name on it and a letter of explanation.

The letter was from the owner of a New York radio

station, who had thrown the bottle into the sea nearly ten months earlier as a way to celebrate the station's twenty-fifth year of broadcasting.

Miguel's name, the letter went on to say, and the way he had found the bottle would be written up in a newspaper story. Could the priest send a picture of Miguel holding the check?

The old priest and Miguel laughed and hugged each other. The treasure bottle had not been a hoax. It had made Miguel the richest boy in the Azores Islands!

A Variety
of Useful Services

For as long as men and ships have sailed the waters of the earth, seagoing bottles have performed a variety of useful services.

They have charted unknown seas, solved mysteries, and revealed crimes. They have delivered messages for spies, brought criminals to justice, patched up quarrels between lovers, and brought romance to people thousands of miles apart. They have spread the Gospel, brought comfort to the troubled, tracked schools of fish, and predicted the course of oil spills. They have carried wills, caused lawsuits, and promised enormous fortunes. By tracking drifting mines powerful enough to blow a ship out of the water, they have saved countless lives. Reading a bottle message in England was once a

15

crime punishable by death. More than once seagoing bottles have proved the old saying that truth is stranger than fiction.

For centuries, bottles have carried messages from doomed men—and not only from men on sinking ships.

On February 1, 1916, during World War I, the German airship *Zeppelin L-19* dropped bombs on London and was in turn hit by British antiaircraft guns. On the trip home over the North Sea, Captain Odo Loewe and the crew of the zeppelin vanished.

Two months later, a bottle was washed ashore on a German beach. "Our final hour is at hand," read the note inside, and it was signed "Captain Odo Loewe." The message left no doubt about what had happened to the airship on that dark night over a black and stormy sea.

For years, passengers on ocean liners have tossed bottles into the sea with checks enclosed and messages asking the finder to write a letter saying where the bottle was found.

In 1927, after Charles Lindbergh had flown across the Atlantic, an American tourist aboard the *President Roosevelt* wrote "Hurrah for Lindbergh!" on a sheet of notepaper and attached a large check to it. He rolled both of them into a bottle and flung the bottle into the *Roosevelt's* wake.

Months later the bottle was found, and the check was

cashed, by a French dress designer in Saffi, Morocco. She had found the bottle bobbing against a stone wall in the harbor.

So dependable are currents off Florida that sailors, passing by on cargo ships, sometimes trust their letters to the sea. One seaman, with a sudden hunger for a sailor's dish called lobscouse (a kind of stew), wrote a letter to the Seamen's Church Institute in New York and asked for the recipe. He applied a stamp, sealed the letter in a bottle, and dropped it into the sea on a Saturday afternoon. At the time, his ship was passing Fort Lauderdale, and the bottle was gently deposited there on a public beach. Someone picked it up and mailed the letter. Ten days later, the seaman's ship docked at Galveston, Texas. There a letter from the Seaman's Church Institute was waiting for him. The recipe for lobscouse was inside.

"A drifting bottle has a birth notice and an obituary," said an oceanographer, "but not a biography."

By this he meant that oceanographers who use bottles to track ocean currents know where a bottle was dropped into the ocean and where it was recovered. What they usually don't know is what happened to the bottle in between those two events.

Oceanographers say bottles are among the most seaworthy objects to travel the oceans. They have bobbed through hurricanes, waited out week-long calms, and survived crushing Arctic ice packs. Some bottle

17

messengers have zipped along on the Gulf Stream at 4 miles per hour covering a hundred miles in a single day.

Generally, a bottle takes twelve to fourteen months to drift between the east coast of the United States and Europe. But one speedster, dropped by scientists into the Mississippi River at New Orleans, drifted into the Gulf of Mexico. It was caught up by the Gulf Stream and carried north up the eastern coast of the United States. Then it moved east across the North Atlantic and beached on the Isle of Wight off England. It had traveled four thousand miles in just ten months.

· 2 ·

True Tales
of Messages Found
in Seagoing Bottles

The Twelve Million Dollar Note

A king's ransom in a bottle? It happened. One man found what was possibly the single most valuable piece of paper ever placed inside a bottle and set adrift on the world's oceans.

On March 16, 1949, Jack Wurm was walking along the shore of the Pacific Ocean near San Francisco. Mr. Wurm was fifty-five years old. He worked as a dishwasher in a restaurant.

Seeing a bottle washed up on the beach, he picked it up, pulled the cork, and removed a rolled-up square of brown wrapping paper. Much to his amazement, the handwritten note read:

To avoid all confusion, I leave my entire estate

to the lucky person who finds this bottle and to my lawyer, Barry Cohen, share and share alike.

Daisy Alexander
June 20, 1937

Wurm didn't believe the note. Who would write a will and set it adrift in a bottle? The very idea was silly. And who would leave money and property worth anything to a complete stranger—whoever found the bottle? Wurm laughed. Well, it made a good story.

A few weeks later he told a friend about the bottle. But to Wurm's surprise, his friend didn't think the story funny at all.

"Don't you know who Daisy Alexander was?" the friend said. "Only one of the world's richest women, that's all!"

He told Wurm that Daisy Alexander was the only child of Isaac Singer, the American sewing-machine millionaire. She had died in 1940 at the age of eighty years. Although married, Mrs. Alexander had had no children. Newspapers reported that, when she died, she left $12 million in money and property, but that a will she had made a few years before her death was never found. Her lawyer in England had been trying for years to find it. He had even hired clairvoyants, people who claimed they were in touch with the spirits of dead people, to find it.

"I was in England and the story was in all the papers,"

22

Wurm's friend said. "If I were you, I'd follow up on it. Maybe you've found the missing will!"

Wurm wrote a letter to "Postmaster, London, England." In his letter he told about finding the bottle and the note and asked the postmaster to find the lawyer, Barry Cohen.

The postmaster did as Wurm asked. Over the next several months, letters went back and forth across the Atlantic between Wurm and Cohen.

Cohen said that the scrap of paper might indeed be Mrs. Alexander's missing will. She had been a lady known for doing strange things. For years she had gone to a bridge over the Thames River in the heart of London and dropped bottles into the water. "I like to see where they turn up," she told a friend.

The bottle that Wurm found, Cohen said, could have been carried by the Thames out to the English Channel, where it went north into the North Sea. From there it could have traveled west across the top of the world through the polar ice pack. Then it might have drifted south through the Bering Strait and along the coasts of Alaska, Canada, Washington, Oregon, and California. Finally, nearly twelve years after Mrs. Alexander sent the bottle on its voyage, it had drifted ashore near San Francisco.

Did Wurm ever get the money?

At last report, five years after Wurm had found the bottle, he was still washing dishes in the same restaurant and lawyers were still arguing the case in London courts.

"There are a lot of hurdles to go over when a guy picks up a bottle on a beach and stakes a claim for millions just on the strength of a piece of paper in that bottle," Wurm told a reporter. "I don't know what's been happening. To tell you the truth, I'm afraid to let myself think much about the matter."

The Blank Check
in the Jam Jar

One day early in 1956, Martin Douglas told his wife, Alice, he was going fishing for the day, and put out to sea for Miami, Florida, in his small cabin cruiser. That night he did not return, and Mrs. Douglas called the police. Despite an air and sea search, neither Martin Douglas nor his boat was ever seen again.

A year later, on a beach in Australia, on the other side of the world from Miami, a man found a jam jar with the lid tightly closed. Inside was a note.

"Should this note be found," it read, "please forward it to my wife, Mrs. Alice Douglas, at Miami Beach, Florida. No doubt you're wondering what has become of me. I got blown out into the waters due to engine trouble."

Accompanying the note was a blank check. On the back of the check was a handwritten will—the last act of a thoughtful man who knew the end of his life was near.

The Ship
That Turned Turtle

In 1902, the S.S. *Huronian* left Glasgow, Scotland, bound for Newfoundland. Weeks passed, but the cargo ship never arrived at its destination.

For two months, U.S. Navy ships searched the North Atlantic. The *Huronian* was never found. The navy's final report: "Lost at sea."

Then, months after the search ended, a bottle drifted ashore on a rocky beach in Nova Scotia. The handwritten message inside read:

"Huronian turned turtle in Atlantic Sunday night. Fourteen of us in a boat."

Navy investigators knew that "turned turtle" was a seaman's term for a ship turning over. But the note was unsigned. Was it a hoax? Investigators thought it might be.

As strange as it may seem, bottles with *fake* messages about ship sinkings are sometimes found. Investigators are always on the watch for them. Insurance claims—money paid to the owner of a ship or to relatives of missing seamen—might depend on what a note says.

In 1909, for example, the *Waratah* vanished in the long stretch of empty ocean between South Africa and Australia.

Over the next few years, more than a dozen letters about the *Waratah* came to Lloyd's of London, the best-known marine-insurance company in the world.

With these letters, writers enclosed notes signed by members of the *Waratah*'s crew. They claimed that they had found the notes in bottles that had drifted ashore.

But the insurance company said all the notes were hoaxes—fakes. No two notes gave the same story about what had happened to the *Waratah*. The notes were also too long and too complete. No seaman on a sinking ship would sit down and carefully write out all the details of what was happening.

Insurance investigators also checked the handwriting of the notes with relatives of the missing crew members. The writing was never the same as in other letters the seamen had sent.

Where did the senders of the letters get the names of *Waratah* crew members? From newspaper stories about the missing ship that listed seamen's names.

Why did these people take the time to write out letters and sign them with the names of dead seamen? Investigators can say only that some people have a strange sense of humor, a creepy kind of humor, that delights in other people's misfortune.

As for the *Huronian,* though, the letter that had washed ashore near Owl's Head proved not to be a hoax. Five years later, another bottle was found, this one on the other side of the Atlantic near a seacoast village in northern Scotland. A note in the second bottle proved the first note genuine.

"Huronian sinking fast," the note read. "Top heavy, one side awash. Goodbye mother and sister—Charlie M'Fell, greaser."

Investigators checked with the owner of the *Huronian.* Yes, a Charles M'Fell had been in the ship's crew. He had worked in the engine room. His main job was to keep the moving parts of the engines greased. The handwriting on the note matched his signature in company records; he did have a mother and sister living in Scotland.

Veteran seamen of the North Atlantic knew then what had happened to the *Huronian.* A sudden storm. The cargo in the hold had shifted as the ship rolled and tossed in the waves. Then a steep wave, and the cargo had tumbled against one side of the ship. The *Huronian* leaned to one side; the deck dipped into the sea.

29

Another tremendous wave and the *Huronian* turned over on her side. The crew had only moments to clamber into boats.

Then came the cold, a slow numbing of the body; they had no food or water. Desperate notes were stuffed into bottles and thrown into the raging sea. Death had come to the seamen before long. Contrary currents eventually carried the bottles to opposite shores of the great ocean.

The five-year-old mystery of what had happened to the *Huronian* had been solved by two drifting bottles.

Torpedoed Off Gibraltar

Two boys playing on a Maine beach in 1947 came upon a tangle of wreckage. Among the cast-up litter they found a corked beer bottle with a note inside.

"Our ship is sinking. The SOS won't help. I guess this is it. Good-bye now—maybe this will reach the good old U.S.A."

The note was signed and at the bottom was scrawled the name and address of a relative.

Navy experts read the note and examined the wreckage. It had come from the U.S. *Beatty*, a Navy destroyer.

On November 6, 1943, the *Beatty* had been torpedoed off Gibraltar at the entrance to the Mediterranean Sea. The loss of life was heavy. The bottle note had taken four years to travel three thousand miles from the scene of the tragic sinking back home to America.

The Man Who Received His Own Death Note Through the Mail

Some tragedies at sea have a happy, if strange, ending, as one bottle message showed.

In 1825, the British sailing ship *Kent* was heading for home when it caught fire in the Bay of Biscay. The huge bay is an arm of the Atlantic indenting the west coast of France and the northern coast of Spain.

Among the passengers on the *Kent* were an English army officer, Major D. W. MacGregor, his wife Elizabeth, and his daughter Joanna.

Certain that the *Kent* was doomed, Major MacGregor wrote the following note, inserted it into a bottle, and threw it far from the burning ship.

"Ship on fire. Elizabeth, Joanna, and myself commit our spirits to the Hands of our Redeemer. Whose grace enables us to be quite composed in the awful prospect of entering Eternity."

The *Kent* burned to the waterline and sank. The bottle, adrift in the Atlantic for the next year and a half, was washed ashore in the Bahamas Islands. A British landowner on the islands found the note and sent it to London. He addressed the letter to Major MacGregor.

How did he know where to send the letter?

Major MacGregor, his wife Elizabeth, and his daughter Joanna were picked up by another British ship, the *Cambria,* along with the *Kent's* other passengers and crew. The *Cambria* had come upon the scene just as the burning *Kent* sank into the sea. Major MacGregor's name and address had appeared in newspaper stories of the sinking, and the man who found the bottle in the Bahamas simply searched through old newspapers until he found the story that listed survivors' names and addresses.

In London, Major MacGregor, alive and well, had the strange experience of reading the last note he had ever expected to write before his life ended.

A Pure Bowshot
at 700 Meters

World War I was less than a year old. At 1:20 P.M. on May 7, 1915, Kapitän-Leutnant Walter Schwieger, commanding the German submarine *U-20,* raised the periscope and peered through the eyepiece. Suddenly he shouted, "Four funnels . . . upward of twenty-five thousand tons, speed about twenty-two knots!"

It was the ship Schwieger had been searching for, the *Lusitania,* at 760 feet and 32,000 tons the largest ocean liner in the world. She was rounding the southern coast of Ireland and was about to head north in the St. George's Channel between Ireland and England.

Fifty minutes later, twelve miles south of Old Head of Kinsale, a steep, rocky cliff jutting into the Atlantic, Schwieger ordered one torpedo fired. The torpedo was set to strike the speeding ship nine feet below the water-line.

"Pure bowshot at seven hundred meters' range," he said for another officer to record in the *U-20's* logbook. "Shot strikes starboard side behind bridge. . . ."

Immediately the huge liner heeled to starboard. The bow dipped and plowed into the sea. In four minutes the foredeck—the front deck on the ship—was under water and green sea poured in through the deck hatches. Water also entered the ship through open portholes in the passengers' cabins on the lower decks. Each minute, 3¾ tons of water poured through each porthole—and there were dozens of these portholes open to the sea.

Fifteen minutes after the torpedo had hit her, the *Lusitania's* bow struck the granite floor of the Atlantic 320 feet below. The weight of the water in the front part of the ship lifted the stern clear of the water. People in the water and in lifeboats could see the huge propellers still slowly turning.

The sun shone and the sea was calm and warm. Only six of the *Lusitania's* forty-eight lifeboats were lowered before the great ship sank. Of the nearly 2000 passengers and crew aboard, 1201 people died; only 764 were saved.

Wreckage from the *Lusitania* floated on the westward tide. In the next few days, two hundred bodies drifted gently ashore on the sands of Garrettstown Strand, on the mudflats of Courtmacsherry Bay, and farther west at Schull, Bantry, and below the rocky headland of the Kerry coast.

Searchers poked through the flotsam of the tides. In one tangle they found a tightly corked champagne bottle with a note inside.

"I am still on deck with a few people. One is a child. The last boats have left. The orchestra is playing bravely. Some men near me are praying with a priest. The end is near. Maybe this note will . . ."

Three years later, in 1918, a second bottle was found half buried in sand and seaweed on a lonely English beach. The note inside was partly decayed from saltwater seeping into the bottle. The note read:

"Lusitania, May 7, 1915. Have been torpedoed. Send help."

Both notes were unsigned. No one knows who aboard the *Lusitania* on that tragic day wrote these notes in the eighteen brief minutes between the moment when the *U-20*'s torpedo struck and the moment when the great ship sank under the waves.

Letter
From a Dead Soldier

Tasmania is a large island, 180 miles long and 190 miles wide, south of Australia. It is separated from the Australian mainland by the Bass Strait, which is about 150 miles wide.

In 1953, a bottle drifted ashore on a narrow Tasmanian beach. Inside was a note written thirty-seven years earlier by two Australian soldiers whose home was in Tasmania. When they wrote the note, the two soldiers were on a troopship bound for the battlefields of France in World War I.

The mother of one soldier was still living and the note was delivered to her. She recognized the handwriting of her son. The young man had been killed in action in France in 1918, thirty-five years before the message reached her.

Bottles
That Came Home

Some bottle messages confirm our belief in how things happen by pure chance. Consider these two messages:

In November 1933, the steamer *Saxilby,* loaded with iron ore, left Ireland and headed into the Atlantic. The *Saxilby* was never heard from again.

"Whatever happened to Joe Okane?" people asked in the seacoast village of Aberayron, Wales. Joe, whose family had lived in Aberayron for years, had been a member of the twenty-five-man crew aboard the *Saxilby.*

Two and a half years later, the people of Aberayron had their answer when a beach walker found a bottle. It lay like a stick on the pebbled beach. Atlantic storm waves, pushed by gale winds, had just washed it ashore. Inside was a note.

"S.S. *Saxilby* sinking off Irish coast," the note read. "Love to sisters, brothers, and Dinah. Joe Okane."

What is strange about the incident is where the sea delivered the message. The pebbled beach was at Aberayron, less than a mile from the doorstep of the people Joe Okane had loved and left behind when he put to sea in the ill-fated *Saxilby*.

The year was 1784, and Chunosuke Matsuyama, a Japanese seaman, and forty-three companions set out on a brave adventure, a search for treasure buried on a Pacific island.

But fate decided that Matsuyama and his friends were not to find the treasure. On the vast ocean, a mighty storm came up. High waves almost turned the small ship over and the sails were ripped. Finally the wind blew the battered craft onto a coral reef. Matsuyama and the other crew members jumped out and waded ashore.

Safe from the raging waves, they gave thanks that they were saved. Or were they?

The next day the storm blew itself out and the sky cleared. Matsuyama and his friends looked around the tiny island now bathed in warm sunlight. The storm had uprooted palm trees. The island was a wreck. Except for a few coconuts, it offered absolutely nothing to eat.

For days the men ate tiny crabs that dashed toward

the surf when any of the starving sailors crept too close. Even so, the crabs they caught were salty and the island had no fresh water to soothe their thirst.

Matsuyama watched his friends die one by one. He realized that none of them, himself included, would ever see their families or their beloved Japan again. But maybe, just maybe, he could send a message home.

In the wreckage of his ship, he found a bottle. Then, using a knife he always carried strapped to his waist, he cut thin pieces of wood from a fallen coconut tree. Carefully he carved a message—the story of what had happened to him and his shipmates. Sealing the wood message tightly into the bottle, he flung it as far as he could and watched as it drifted away on the blue ocean.

That was Matsuyama's last known act. Shortly thereafter he and all his shipmates died of thirst and starvation.

But the bottle survived. For years it drifted on the ocean. Wind and waves pushed it along. Currents carried it this way and that. Storm waves tossed it. Calms that lasted for days held it fixed in one place. And then, in 1935, a century and a half after Matsuyama had set it adrift, the bottle was washed ashore on a narrow beach.

The person who found it was a Japanese seaweed collector. The place where the bottle came ashore was the village of Hiraturemura, the birthplace of Chunosuke Matsuyama, the young men who had gone treasure hunting 151 years before and had never returned.

41

"Your Old Pal, Bill . . ."

In 1934, Doyle Branscum wrote his name and address on the back of a snapshot of himself, slipped it into a bottle, and threw the bottle into a river in Arkansas.

Twenty-four years passed. Branscum had totally forgotten the incident. Then, one day in 1958, he received a letter. In it was the old snapshot taken when he was a boy. But even more amazing was the letter that came with the snapshot. It was signed, "Your old pal, Bill."

The letter came from Branscum's boyhood friend, Bill Headstream, who said that he had found the bottle and snapshot on the beach near his home at Largo, Florida. The two friends hadn't heard from each other since Headstream and his parents had moved away from Arkansas nearly a quarter century before.

Bottle Postmen That Deliver Letters from Lonely Hearts

In May, 1957, Sebastiano Puzzo, a factory worker, was walking along a beach on Sicily.

Sicily is the largest island in the Mediterranean Sea. Shaped roughly like a triangle and almost entirely covered by mountains, it is separated from the "toe" of Italy by the narrow Strait of Messina. On a narrow strip of sand between the mountains and the sea, Puzzo found a bottle with a note inside.

Puzzo could not read English, so he took the note home. "Paolina," he said to his pretty eighteen-year-old daughter. "Look what I found. You studied English in school. Read for me what the note says."

The note was dated December, 1955. It was from

Ake Viking, a sailor on a Swedish ship. Ake's home was in Göteborg, Sweden.

"Listen to this, Father," Paolina said, laughing. "This man is asking all girls aged sixteen to twenty to write to him if they want to marry a handsome blond Swede!"

"Then write to him," Puzzo said, "just as a joke. Send him your picture."

And Paolina did—just as a joke.

Soon Ake visited Sicily. A year after Puzzo found the bottle with Viking's letter, his daughter and the "handsome blond Swede" were married.

On the other side of the world, an ocean liner was docked in an Australian port. A sailor brought a bottle with a message in it to his captain, who read it and handed it to a pretty woman employed as a cabin maid.

"It's for you," he said.

Puzzled, the young woman read the message.

"I am a mate on a freighter bound for the South Seas," it said. "I am a lonesome fellow and hope that fate will bring me a wife. Perhaps somewhere in the Commonwealth there is a girl not older than thirty who wants to write to me."

The mate's name and address were on the bottom of the note. A photograph was clipped to the note.

Months later, two things happened. The captain of the ocean liner lost a good maid, and the lonesome mate gained a wife.

In Miami, Florida, a seaman had an argument with his wife. He stormed out of the house and went to his ship.

A week later, as his ship was about to pass Miami, he wrote a letter to his wife. "Forgive me," he said. "I'm sorry we argued."

He rolled the letter into a cylinder, inserted it in a bottle, and tossed the bottle overboard. Currents pushed the bottle toward the beach. There a swimmer found it and mailed the letter.

Exactly one week after the seaman threw the bottle overboard, his ship docked in New York. There a letter was waiting for him. It was from his wife.

"I forgive you," she wrote.

Christmas night, 1945, was lonely for a U.S. Army serviceman named Frank Hayostek. World War II had ended that year. Hayostek had been away from home for three years. Standing at the rail of a troopship heading for the United States, he stuffed a note into an aspirin bottle. He corked the bottle, taped the top, and tossed it far into the ship's churning wake. The note read:

Dear Finder,

I am an American soldier . . . 21 years old . . . just a plain American of no wealth, but just enough to get along with. This is my third Christmas from home. . . . God bless you.

He signed his name and added his street address in Johnstown, Pennsylvania.

Nine months later in September, 1946, Frank Hayostek, now discharged from the army, received a letter from Ireland. He was puzzled. He didn't know anyone in Ireland.

I have found your bottle and note (the letter said). I will tell you the whole story.

I live on a farm at the southwest coast of Ireland. On Friday, Aug. 23, 1946, I drove the cows to the fields beside the sea and then went for a walk on the strand [beach] called The Beal. It is an inlet of Dingle Bay.

Well, my dog was running before me and I saw him stop and sniff something light on the sand, and then he went off in pursuit of sea gulls. I found the object was a brown bottle. . . . The cork . . . crumpled in my fingers. How the note kept dry, nobody can understand. It must have been because you mentioned God's name on it, and He brought it to safe harbor. . . . I sat there on the beach and read it.

I thought at first I was dreaming. This is just a little common Irish village where nothing strange ever occurs, and this is something for the farmers to talk about while they cut the oats and bring the hay into the barn. Well, imagine, the bottle has been on the sea for eight months. . . . Who knows where it has been? It may have traveled around the world. How did it escape being broken on the rocks? If you had only seen where I got it! It's all a mess of rocks. The hand of Providence must surely have guided it.

Well, I hope to hear from you soon. . . . You mention offering no reward to the finder of the bottle. Well, I ask no reward, as it was a very pleasant surprise. Wishing you very good luck, your loving friend,

Breda O'Sullivan

Over the next seven years, seventy letters traveled across the Atlantic between Breda O'Sullivan in Ireland and Frank Hayostek in Johnstown, Pennsylvania, U.S.A.

Breda was a farm girl in the village of Lispole, County Kerry. She wrote of raising a greyhound, of acting in theater plays in Killarney, and of hoping one day to teach Frank the hornpipe—an Irish dance.

Frank was now working as a welder. He wrote that he had sold his 1941 automobile and was saving $80 each month for a plane ticket to visit Breda in Ireland.

In August 1952, six years after Breda O'Sullivan found his bottle message, Frank Hayostek boarded a plane and flew to Ireland. He took along his best suit.

For Breda, he carried presents of nylon stockings and a music box.

By this time, newspaper reporters had heard about the letters going back and forth between Breda and Frank and how they had started with Hayostek's message in a bottle. Frank and Breda were important news. All across the United States, people followed the bottle-message romance in their daily newspapers.

In Ireland, after Hayostek's plane landed, reporters followed Breda and Frank as they visited the Lakes of Killarney. Later, the two young people spent several hours in the thatched-roof cottage on the O'Sullivan's fifteen-acre farm. Breda, reporters informed their readers, served Frank tea and cakes. The cakes had been especially made by the baker in Dingle.

Much to the couple's embarrassment, newspapers in America and Europe reported on their day together. The question everyone wanted answered was: Would they fall in love and get married?

"It's in the hands of God," answered Frank. "She's very nice."

"After all," said Breda, "we only met a few hours ago. Up to then, he was only a man in a bottle."

A few days later, as reporters waited for a wedding announcement, Breda and Frank decided to end the suspense.

"There is no romance and there will be no wedding," Breda said. "We will remain good pen pals."

And so the grand romance, started when a lonely soldier stuffed a note in a bottle and threw it into the Atlantic, came to an end. Newspaper readers in Europe and America were of course disappointed. Romantic stories like this were supposed to end in marriage!

But Breda O'Sullivan and Frank Hayostek decided not to go along with what the world expected of them. They knew what was right for them. And so the story ended.

Pine Forge Elementary
Boyertown Area Schools

Bottle Preachers Cast the Gospel Upon the Waters

"Bottle preachers" have used bottles to carry the Gospel message to every shore in the world.

In Middlesboro, a small town in the Kentucky mountains, H. Harrison Mayes cleans out whiskey bottles and stuffs them with messages like "Prepare to meet God!" The messages are printed in sixteen languages, including Chinese.

He mails the bottles to friends in other countries. The friends drop the bottles into the ocean.

In 1974, Mayes, who was then seventy-six years old, received a letter from the Philippine Islands. The writer said he had found one of Mayes's bottles. Checking his records, Mayes discovered that the bottle had been thrown into the ocean off Nicaragua in Central America twenty-three years before.

Bottle Preachers Cast the Gospel Upon the Waters

Another bottle preacher was the Reverend Jewel Pierce of Piedmont, Alabama. Between 1946 and 1955, Reverend Pierce threw thirty thousand bottles into a stream flowing into the Alabama River, which in turn flows into the Gulf of Mexico at Mobile. Each bottle carried a sermon. The Reverend Pierce never said how many replies he had received in response to his messages.

A bottle preacher who did talk about the answers he received was Brother George Phillips of Tacoma, Washington. In 1940, Brother George began collecting whiskey and wine bottles from trash cans at the back doors of saloons. In the next twenty years, he launched fifteen thousand bottles into Puget Sound, whose currents carried them into the Pacific Ocean.

Each bottle contained a message warning readers of the evils of strong drink, a problem Brother George knew well. He had fought a drinking problem himself—and won.

Over these same years, Brother George claimed he received fourteen hundred replies. Most of the letters came from cities and towns along the Pacific coast and Mexico, but he also received letters from as far away as Hawaii, New Guinea, and Australia.

Of every ten replies, seven carried promises to stop drinking, Brother George said. Another two carried the vows of people who promised to return to church. The remaining letters were from people who wanted

Brother George to know where and when his messages were found.

The most dramatic letter came from a Chicago businessman. Whiskey had ruined him, he wrote. He had lost his business and his wife had left him. Discouraged, he had fled to Mexico.

One day, on a beach near Acapulco, he picked up one of Brother George's bottles. The message ended with the words, "Be sure your sins will find you out!"

The message shook the man. He felt it was directed right to him. He wrote to Brother George. "I am returning to Chicago," he said. "I am going to remake my life."

Two years later, Brother George received a second letter from the man. He was working hard seven days a week to pay off his debts, and his wife had come back to him. He ended by saying: "I owe it all to that bottle that came out of the sea."

Queen Elizabeth's Official Uncorker of Ocean Bottles!

The Strait of Dover, only twenty-one miles wide at its narrowest point, separates England and France and connects the English Channel with the North Sea. Naval battles have been fought there. In the thirteenth century, English ships repelled a French invasion, and in 1588, a huge Spanish fleet—the Spanish Armada—took its first blows from a smaller English fleet in the strait and was in time destroyed.

One day in 1560, a fisherman was rowing beneath the gray chalk cliffs of Dover. At the top of the cliffs stood old forts and castles. At their base, waves washed into caves and tunnels, which smugglers used to hide gunpowder and treasure.

But today the boatman was not interested in the

sights around Dover. His keen eye had caught the glint of sun on a bottle. Eagerly he plucked it from the water. Yes, there was a message inside. He pulled it out.

Delighted at his find, he took the bottle and the message to the chief naval officer at Dover. If the message was important, maybe—just maybe—he would get a gold piece.

After the naval officer had read the message, he glared at the fisherman. "Do you know what this is?"

The fisherman was startled. "Y-yes," he said. "I mean n-no!" Suddenly he wished he had never seen the bottle.

"A message! A *secret* message to her Majesty the Queen!"

The fisherman's mouth gaped. The Queen! Now he was really frightened. He clutched his cap to his chest. "Sir, I—I didn't know!"

The officer leaned across the table. "I do not believe you! You are lying! It says plainly here on the message, 'For the Queen! Not to be read by any other person!' You are in trouble, my man!"

"Good sir, I tell the truth. I do not know what the message says." He lowered his eyes. "I cannot read."

There was silence. The officer glared at the man. Then he sat down in his chair. "Guard! Take this man to a cell. Hold him until we get further orders!"

What the poor fisherman didn't know was that the bottle had been dropped into the Strait of Dover by an English spy. The spy, who was on a Dutch ship sailing south on the strait, had wanted to get an important message to Queen Elizabeth. A bottle was the only way to send the message. Currents in the narrow strait delivered the message for him.

In London, Queen Elizabeth read the message to her councilors. "The Dutch have taken an island in the Arctic Ocean from the Russians and will use it as a naval base. Our ship captains must be warned of this, otherwise they will be captured."

Her advisers nodded agreement.

"But there is something else important here," she added. "Anyone who finds a state message in a bottle might read it. This we cannot permit! Henceforth, it will be an offense against the Crown—punishable by hanging—for anyone to read a message found in a bottle. All bottles must be delivered, unopened, to the palace. Here they will be opened only by my Official Uncorker of Ocean Bottles, a new post, which you, my lord"—she pointed to one man at the table— "will fill!"

From that time on, anyone in England who found a bottle with a message inside delivered it to the authorities. They in turn sent it to London by special messenger on horseback.

And what about the poor fisherman who had found the bottle and started all the fuss, the man who had expected a reward and instead was thrown into a prison cell?

The fact that he couldn't read saved him. When his cell was opened, he quickly ran back to his boat and never again looked for floating bottles.

However, if you are ever walking along an English beach and find a bottle with a message inside, go ahead and read it. You won't be hanged. Queen Elizabeth's law, along with the title of Official Uncorker of Ocean Bottles, was removed from the books in 1760 when George III became king.

The Bottle Message That Called Out the French Navy

November, 1875. The tide flowed from the Bay of Biscay into the tiny harbor of Les Sables d'Olonne on the French coast. A French naval lieutenant, his uniform unbuttoned at the neck, stood with one boot on a low stone wall enjoying the thin autumn sunshine and smoking a cigar. His gaze wandered among the fishing boats and coal scows; then his eyes narrowed. Among the garbage scum floating against the wall was a bottle. And, yes, in the bottle was a note. He could see it from where he stood.

Minutes later he was standing at the desk of his commanding officer. His uniform coat was buttoned.

"Sir, you must read this for yourself! I have no idea if it is true!"

The commanding officer, a full captain in the French navy, unfolded the note. A moment later, he raised his gray eyebrows and looked at the lieutenant. *"Mon Dieu!* If this is true, the crime happened but a few days ago!"

"But could it be a hoax?"

The captain looked out the window. The sun glinted on the water and reflected on the ceiling. "It very well could be! But we are compelled to investigate!"

"The *Tirailleur* is ready, sir."

"Good! Assemble a company of marines and take her. Find the *Lennie* if you can. See if there is any truth in this monstrous story!"

The note that had shocked the two officers told of a mutiny a few days earlier in the Bay of Biscay aboard the British full-rigger *Lennie.* "The crew revolted against the ship's officers," the note read. "They have murdered the captain and two officers. The cabin boy and I have locked ourselves in the saloon."

The note was signed: "Van Hoydek, Ship's Steward."

Within a few days, the *Tirailleur* found the *Lennie.* French marines boarded the British ship, made prisoners of the mutineers, and released Van Hoydek and the cabin boy from the saloon.

The *Tirailleur* took the mutineers to London, where they were placed on trial in a court called the Old Bailey. Van Hoydek, who was a Dutch citizen, told what had happened aboard the *Lennie*. As a result of his testimony, four of the mutineers were hanged.

London newspapers reported the trials, and Van Hoydek became a hero. He was so popular that people gave money into a fund for him.

Did Van Hoydek ever think of the bottle that he had thrown out a porthole in a desperate call for help? The bottle and its message had not only revealed a crime on the high seas that might otherwise have gone undiscovered, but had called out the French navy!

The answer to this question will never be known. After the trial in the Old Bailey, Van Hoydek took the money the public had given him and opened a restaurant in Wapping. The restaurant became very popular. He married an English girl and never went to sea again.

Two Cats
on a Ghost Ship

The day was January 31, 1921, a wet, misty morning. At Diamond Shoals, North Carolina, long gray waves rolled ashore. Hissing and foaming, they spread fanlike on the beach.

At the U.S. Coast Guard station, a young sailor sipped his morning coffee and looked across the restless sea. Suddenly he leaned forward, squinting to see better. Out of the mist, straight for the outer shoals, sailed a five-masted schooner, all sails set.

The young sailor yelled a warning, useless as it was: "The shoals!" His coffee cup smashed on the floor as he sprang to pull the warning siren. A whooping wail shattered the still morning, but it was too late. The ship lifted as her bow ground on the rising underwater sandbar.

She lurched to one side. Her sails flapped in the light breeze.

Minutes later six coastguardsmen were rowing through the low waves to the stranded ship, the *Carroll A. Deering*. But, oddly, as they approached, no one appeared on deck.

The coastguardsmen climbed aboard. Not only was the ship without a crew, they discovered, but her motor lifeboat and dory were gone. Her charts, log, and navigating instruments were also missing. The only living things aboard the ship were two cats that mewed and rubbed against the legs of the sailors.

"If only they could talk!" a Coast Guard officer said. "They could tell us what happened."

Investigation revealed that the *Deering* had left Barbados, West Indies, for Norfolk, Virginia, on January 9, 1921. But why had the crew abandoned the *Deering*? The ship was seaworthy and showed no damage. Besides—something really strange—the cargo was gone. No crew leaving a ship would take along the freight it was carrying.

The Coast Guard could find no answer to these questions, and finally, it closed the investigation. "Unsolved!" was stamped on the file.

And then, on April 11, ten weeks after the *Deering* ran aground, a stroller on the beach at Buxton, North Carolina, came upon a bottle partly covered by sand. Inside was a note, and suddenly the mystery of the

The Twelve Million Dollar Note

Carroll A. Deering was solved.

"*Deering* captured by oil-burning boat something like chaser," it read, "taking off everything, handcuffing crew. Crew hiding all over ship. No chance to make escape. Finder please notify headquarters of *Deering*."

The note was unsigned, but government handwriting experts said the writing was that of Henry Bates of Islesboro, Maine, one of the *Deering*'s crew members. Reviewing the note and the condition of the ship, Coast Guard officers could finally say what had probably happened aboard the *Deering*.

Ships loading cargo at Barbados sometimes took aboard cases of unlawful whiskey for sale in the United States. A ship as big as the *Deering* could carry whiskey worth a million dollars or more. Its entire cargo was probably whiskey and no other freight.

Somewhere near the United States coast, gangsters, using small but powerful World War I submarine-patrol ships, boarded the *Deering*. They murdered the crew and cut the lifeboats adrift to make it look as if the crew had left the ship. Then they moved the cargo of whiskey to their own boats. They left the *Deering*'s sails set. Winds drove the ship toward shore.

The cats had witnessed the terrible crime, but they of course could tell nothing. Coast Guard officers agreed that the case was solved. The bottle note had indeed solved the mystery of the ghost ship *Carroll A. Deering*.

"Five Ponies, 150 Dogs Remaining . . ."

On his last expedition to the Arctic in 1901-1902, the famous explorer Evelyn Baldwin became lost. His party's supplies were nearly gone when Baldwin wrote a note in both Norwegian and English, placed it in a bottle, and threw it into the Arctic Ocean.

Forty-seven years later, a Russian fisherman found the bottle on the edge of an ice pack near Vilkitski Strait. Unable to read the message, he took it to Murmansk. There, authorities read:

"Five ponies and 150 dogs remaining. Desire hay, fish, and 30 sledges. Must return early in August." It was signed "Evelyn Baldwin."

How the bottle survived nearly half a century without being crushed in drifting ice packs is a mystery. But survive it did. What was not a mystery was what had happened to Evelyn Baldwin and his men. The explorer had led his party safely out of the Arctic and to the United States. He died in 1933—in bed at his home in New York—sixteen years before his desperate message was found by the Russian fisherman.

Cape Sheridan, 1905: Peary Was Here!

Another Arctic explorer who placed a message in a bottle was Commander Robert Peary, an American naval officer who, in 1909, was the first man to reach the North Pole.

Before his discovery, however, Peary had made an earlier try at reaching "90 north," the geographical top of the world.

In the fall of 1905, Peary's ship *Roosevelt* nosed into Robeson Channel off Cape Sheridan, Ellesmere Island, Canada, 550 miles south of the Pole.

As he walked up the rocky shore, Peary came upon a cairn—a mound of stones or rock. Arctic explorers often built cairns and left bottle messages in them to prove they had actually visited a particular place. This cairn

held a letter from Sir George Nares, an earlier English explorer. Nares had visited the Arctic with a British expedition in 1875-1976.

Peary took Nare's letter, made a copy, and placed it in a whiskey bottle in a new cairn. With the copy, he placed a letter that told about his own expedition.

Peary did not reach the Pole on that attempt. However, when he returned to the Arctic four years later, he reached the North Pole by another route.

Meanwhile, Peary's handwritten report of his 1905 expedition stayed safely in the cairn on Cape Sheridan through forty-three severe winters. Then, in the late summer of 1948, twenty-eight years after Peary died, three Canadian and United States ships entered the same waters off Cape Sheridan, carrying food and supplies for weather-station crews deep in the Arctic wilderness.

Naval officers on the ships knew of Peary's cairn and were on the lookout for it. A weatherman, Charles Hubbard, was the first to see it. The cairn was marked with a wooden cross. On the cross Peary had marked a large *R* for his ship *Roosevelt*. Hubbard took apart the mound of flat shale. Inside he found an old Scotch-whisky bottle. In it was the letter Peary had written forty-three years earlier.

Hubbard took the bottle back to his ship. There he made copies of both Peary's letter and Sir George Nares's letter. Ice was getting thick in Robeson Chan-

nel, so Hubbard used a helicopter to fly back to Cape Sheridan, where he built a new cairn. In it he placed another bottle that held copies of both Peary's and Nares' letters.

The bottle may still be there today holding its letters safe from the cruel polar weather, waiting for the next Arctic traveler to come along.

· 3 ·

Charting
Ocean Currents
with Seagoing Bottles

The letter, sent from Milton, Florida, was dated July 22, 1974. It was addressed to Texas A&M University, Department of Civil Engineering, College Station, Texas.

Dear Sir [it read]. For many years, since I was a child in California, I have looked for a bottle in the ocean with a message in it. On Sunday, July 7th, my son and his wife and I were walking on the beach about 6:30 p.m. I had picked up several bottles on the beach and in the water and kept saying, "No message in this one."

Then my son picked up the bottle containing the card enclosed. The cap on the bottle was rusty and the card saturated with salt water. I saved as much as possible. The approximate location was 3 miles west of Navarre Beach Fishing Pier, Florida. If it is at all possible I would like to know when & where the bottle was put in the water and approximately what date. I would be interested in more information about the survey.

Letters like this come every year to oceanographers—scientists who study the oceans—in a half dozen universities and oceanographic institutions in the United States. They come from people who find bottles with postcards inside. The postage-paid, self-addressed cards ask the finder to report where and when the bottle was found and then mail it.

By charting where a bottle was dropped into the water and where it was found, oceanographers can trace its passage in the ocean. Hundreds of cards over a period of many years help oceanographers chart the streams and rivers in the sea that we call currents. Oceanographers today use several devices to follow ocean currents—plastic drifters, cards sealed in plastic bags, and weighted drifters that meander along the sea floor to follow bottom currents. But seagoing bottles are the most widely used current-tracking device, and certainly the oldest.

The First
Oceanographers

The first oceanographer to use bottles to track currents was a Greek, Theophrastus (c. 372–c. 287 B.C.). He believed that the Mediterranean Sea received most of its water from the Atlantic Ocean. Two thousand years ago, he asked Greek ship captains to drop sealed bottles at the Strait of Gibraltar, the 8-mile-wide (at its narrowest point) western entrance to the Mediterranean. In time, many of these bottles passed through the narrow strait and drifted east for the entire length of the Mediterranean, proving Theophrastus' theory.

Someone else who was curious about ocean currents was America's Benjamin Franklin.

Franklin was interested in many things—painting, law, electricity—but ocean currents held a special fascination for him.

Long before the War of Independence, Franklin was deputy postmaster general of the colonies. One day, in 1769, a group of Boston shop owners came to him with a complaint.

"Mr. Franklin," they said, "why must English ships take two weeks longer than our American ships to cross the Atlantic with the mail? It's the same ocean, isn't it? English ships hold up business!"

Franklin talked to his cousin, Timothy Folger, who was also captain of a New England whaling ship. "It's true," Folger said. "Yankee captains ride the Gulf Stream going east. Coming home, though, they avoid sailing against it. It's like sailing upstream!"

Franklin asked why English captains didn't use the swift current of the Gulf Stream to speed their eastward crossing and why they didn't avoid sailing against it coming to America.

Folger shrugged. "We have informed them that they were stemming a current that was against them to the value of three miles an hour, but they are too wise to be counseled by simple American fishermen!"

Franklin asked his cousin to draw the Gulf Stream on a chart of the Atlantic. Over the next few years he sent corked bottles drifting on the swiftly flowing ocean current. Notes in the bottles asked finders to write and tell him where they had found a bottle—the same method oceanographers use today.

Once Franklin had double-checked the course of the

Gulf Stream, he sent copies of the chart to Falmouth, England. He hoped English captains would use the chart and take less time to carry the mail to America.

Did English ship captains use Franklin's chart?

"They slighted it!" Franklin said. The English refused to believe that a Yankee postmaster knew more about ocean currents than they did. Yet the chart that Franklin developed of the Gulf Stream is hardly changed today.

Another person interested in the Atlantic's currents was Albert I (1848–1922), Prince of Monaco, a tiny country on the Mediterranean coast near the French-Italian border. World famous as an oceanographer, Albert used four royal yachts to study deep-ocean life. He also asked captains of his yachts to drop bottles carrying cards overboard at certain places in the Atlantic. Between 1885 and 1888, they dropped 1,700 bottles into the ocean.

During the next ten years, 227 cards were mailed back to Albert. Knowing where the bottles had been dropped and where they were recovered, Albert would draw some of the earliest charts of the Atlantic's currents.

Great Ocean Rivers

"Some of these currents," said one of today's oceanographers, "make the Mississippi River look like a mere brook!"

Over many years, oceanographers have discovered that most currents in the Northern Hemisphere—like mighty whirlpools—move clockwise. In the Southern Hemisphere, they usually move counterclockwise. Steady winds and the earth's eastward rotation turn the restless sea in these opposite directions.

In both hemispheres, currents carry warm water away from the equator toward the polar regions. After mixing with cold polar water, the currents turn and flow toward the equator, gradually warming again, to complete the circle.

As they charted these great planetary currents, oceanographers also realized that, within these great ocean rivers, smaller streams flowed that didn't follow regular patterns. The heat of the sun at different times of the year and shifting winds altered the flow of the water.

Scientists realized that trying to chart the exact path of currents was impractical. In 1928, for example, oceanographers dropped ten bottles into the Atlantic at St. Peter and St. Paul Rocks near the equator, halfway between South America and Africa. Out of the ten, two were recovered. One had drifted east to Africa. The second had drifted west to Nicaragua in Central America.

At another time, two bottles were tossed overboard from a ship in the mid-Atlantic. Both bottles ended up on a French beach 350 days later, only yards apart. Together they had journeyed across half an ocean.

Oceanographers have found that, generally, it takes about twelve months for a bottle to drift from the east coast of the United States across the Atlantic to Europe. In the Pacific, a bottle requires about eighteen months to drift from the west coast of Mexico to the Philippine Islands.

The Ends of the Earth

Some extraordinary voyages have been made by seagoing bottles.

● A bottle dropped into the sea from the S.S. *Den of Ruthven* near Cape Horn, South America, on May 31, 1909, was recovered on the west coast of New Zealand on May 13, 1912, a drift of 10,250 miles in three years.

● Six years after an officer aboard a Standard Fruit Company ship dropped a bottle overboard in the Caribbean Sea, a fourteen-year-old Welsh boy found it washed ashore. Oceanographers estimated it had drifted some 13,000 miles.

● The longest-known bottle voyage was the "Flying Dutchman." In 1929, German scientists launched a bottle in the Indian Ocean halfway between the Kerguélen Islands and Tasmania. Inside, clearly readable through the glass, was a message in several languages. The message asked the finder to report where and when the bottle was found, then to throw it back into the sea unopened.

A west-flowing current carried the Flying Dutchman to its first port-of-call, the southern tip of South America near Cape Horn. There it drifted ashore several times, was reported, and tossed back into the sea. Then a current caught it and carried it away from land.

From Cape Horn, it drifted east across the Atlantic back to the Indian Ocean. It passed the spot where the German scientists had dropped it into the sea and drifted on to the west coast of Australia.

There it was picked up on a beach in 1935. The German scientists calculated that, by this time, the bottle had traveled 16,800 miles in 2,447 days, an average drift of seven miles per day.

But, sadly, the Australian landing was the last anyone ever saw of the Flying Dutchman. It was never reported again. For all anyone knows it could be stranded today on a beach in an isolated cove, perhaps buried in sand. Or just possibly it could still be bobbing along, day in and day out, braving storms and calms, over the planet's vast seas.

Long before the Flying Dutchman, however, scientists working with the British Royal Navy began using bottles to chart ocean currents. About 1860, officers on

British ships began dropping bottles overboard at certain places in the oceans. Thirty years later, the U.S. Navy adopted the same program, except that bottles were dropped wherever a ship was at noon. Cards in the bottles were printed in eight languages—English, French, German, Dutch, Italian, Spanish, Portuguese, and Esperanto.

Over many years, an average of 2 to 8 percent of all cards were returned—about 350 cards a year. Most of the bottles drifted between nine months and two years, at an average speed of a half mile per hour, before they were washed ashore. Journeys of 4,000 to 6,000 miles were not uncommon. The longest journey recorded by U.S. Navy oceanographers was 10,250 miles.

Plotting the track of individual bottles enabled the U.S. Navy Hydrographic Office to determine the speed and direction of currents and to chart lanes of fast-moving currents for ships to use. A ship taking advantage of the Gulf Stream, for example, could add two to four knots to its own speed, a saving in time and fuel.

Much Useful Information

    A careful recording of the tracks of bottles over many years has provided much useful information to people who work on the sea.

    For example, in 1894, the Scottish Fishery Board hired scientists to study the currents of the North Sea. Was there any way, the Board wanted to know, that bottles might follow schools of fish moving with a current and thus help fishermen locate more fish to catch? The scientists released 2,074 bottles and 1,479 wooden floats. The bottles and floats followed schools of fish so closely that, in one season, fishing boats following the bottles increased their catch by several tons. The next season, however, storms and high winds made it impossible to follow the bottles.

American oceanographers tried to help United States fishermen in the same way. To enable them to follow the movements of cod and haddock, they dropped bottles among fish eggs floating on the surface. If the eggs drifted toward the open sea—followed by the sentrylike bottles—then so did the mature fish. Or if the bottles drifted over the usual fishing grounds, that was where the adult fish were likely to turn up.

That was the theory, but in practice it didn't work out. Though the method was partly successful, and on a few occasions saved valuable time locating schools of fish, oceanographers found that conflicting currents often separated the bottles and failed to reveal where the fish were.

In another fishing season, bottles helped to solve a mystery—why fishermen couldn't catch any fish. During the previous year their nets had been filled. That year they were empty. What had happened to the fish?

"Every few years," an oceanographer said, "the cod or haddock seemed to disappear. No one knew what happened to them. It was assumed that they migrated somewhere. But the bottles gave a different answer. They showed that a storm in the spawning season created currents that swept the whole crop of fish eggs out to deep water, where they died. Consequently, in some years, there were just no fish to catch."

A few years ago, fishermen complained that garbage and other wastes dumped from barges into the ocean near Long Island were polluting the water and driving fish away. To test the charge, scientists at Woods Hole Oceanographic Institution released several thousand bottles at the waste-dumping site. Neither the wastes nor the bottles drifted to the fishing grounds, the scientists reported. The fish just weren't biting that year.

When an engineer became concerned that a new sewer pipe discharging into the Atlantic off Long Island might pollute swimming beaches, he checked with Woods Hole. Drift bottles revealed that the outlet was too close to land. "We advised him to move the mouth of the pipe farther out or the sewage would end up on the beach right in the middle of the swimming season," an oceanographer reported.

Bottles solved another problem for swimmers in Massachusetts. A few years ago, residents of seaside towns avoided swimming in the ocean when thousands of jellyfish, bell-shaped sea animals usually found in tropical waters, appeared in the shallow water off beaches. The jellyfish's long, trailing tentacles carry poisonous barbs that inflict painful—sometimes deadly—wounds to swimmers who brush against them.

Officials in these towns were worried. Where had the plague of jellyfish come from? What could be done about them? Would the beaches have to be closed?

Oceanographers using drift-bottle data and weather reports solved the problem. The appearance of the jellyfish off Massachusetts was an accident, they said. The jellyfish, pushed by strong winds, had "sailed" northwest to Massachusetts from the Bahamas Islands.

83

Cold northern waters soon solved the problem for the town officials. Accustomed to warm tropical waters, the invaders became chill and died.

Bottles have also proved helpful in tracing sludge oil. This sticky, tarlike mass, blown into the sea by ships cleaning their engines, drifts on currents until it runs ashore and fouls beaches. Many beaches, especially in western Europe, are slowly being ruined by this sludge oil.

Using bottles to trace the route of drifting oil, British scientists found safe places in harbors and inlets where the sludge could be safely disposed of.

The paths of currents tracked by drifting bottles proved helpful after two world wars. At the end of World War I, drifting mines in Europe's waters were a great menace to ships. Seven weeks after the Armistice, Prince Albert of Monaco prepared charts showing where ships could sail to avoid currents that carried mines.

After World War II, Japanese mines drifting in the Pacific sank many ships. By charting the tracks of thousands of drift bottles dropped in the water long before the war by both Japan and the United States, it was possible to establish "green" lanes that were free of mines and "red" lanes where mines were most likely to be found. How many lives the floating bottles saved by helping to reroute ships from "red" lanes can never be estimated.

Private Groups

The United States Government no longer engages in a drift-bottle program. But private oceanographic institutions and universities, such as Woods Hole Oceanographic Institution, the University of Michigan, Florida State University, the Scripps Institute of Oceanography, and Texas A&M University, to mention some, continue the work. The United States Government, however, does still "archive [store] the data which other institutions collect," said a spokesman for the National Oceanographic Data Center, U.S. Department of Commerce.

After years of gathering data from drift bottles, Woods Hole assembled an atlas of current patterns titled *Surface Circulation on the Continental Shelf off* ·

Eastern North America between Newfoundland and Florida. Useful to fishermen, scientists, and the captains of ocean liners, cargo ships, and racing yachts, the atlas presents a chart of currents for each season and each month of the year.

At Texas A&M University, Dr. Wesley P. James, Department of Civil Engineering, headed a research team that charted currents near the coastline on the Gulf of Mexico.

"Most suitable current studies," Dr. James said, "have been done out in deep water. We know quite a lot about currents and temperatures past the thirty-mile mark or so, but we know very little about currents that are close to shore. By using the information furnished by those who find the bottles, we can map shoreline currents with reasonable accuracy."

One result of the study Dr. James and his group made was to mark on charts where oil would drift if an oil spill occurred thirty miles out in the Gulf off Freeport, Texas. There a terminal is located at which big tankers tie up to unload their cargo of oil and have it pumped ashore. By anticipating where the oil would drift in the event of an accidental spill, cleanup could be hastened and damage to shorelines lessened.

Between July and September, 1973, Dr. James and his team released 930 drift bottles, each five inches high and weighted with sand so it would barely float (to minimize the push of sea winds). A year later, 269 had been returned—about 30 percent.

"I wrote each person a letter explaining a little of the project," Dr. James said. "I think most people were happy to help with a scientific experiment."

A state agency interested in drift-bottle research is the South Carolina Wildlife and Marine Resources Department, Charleston, South Carolina. This agency used a research vessel, the *Dolphin,* to drop bottles every two months at seventy-seven different places in the Gulf of Mexico between Georgetown, South Carolina, and Cape Lookout, North Carolina.

This study was designed to help fishermen predict the year's catch of menhaden, a kind of herring used to make a nutritious food for farm animals. Menhaden spawn at sea. After hatching, the tiny fish then ride ocean currents ashore to inlets where they grow and mature. If currents drift toward shore, the following year's catch of adult menhaden will be good. If they don't, the catch will be light. By following currents, bottles help to predict the coming year's catch.

Recovery

Of the thousands of bottles scientists release at sea to track currents, how many are actually recovered?

Data for the Woods Hole atlas came from 156,276 bottles dropped into the ocean between 1948 and 1962. The bottles were dropped from oil-drilling rigs, Coast Guard patrol ships and planes, ferry boats, blimps, lightships along the East Coast, ocean-research vessels, International Ice Patrol Unit ships tracking icebergs, weather ships, and private yachts. The total return was 11 percent, of which 17,024 bottles were recovered along the Atlantic coast and 356 came from overseas.

In another project carried on between 1960 and 1970, Woods Hole scientists released 165,566 bottles off the east coast of the United States. By September of 1971, 16,432 had been recovered from North American shores and another 115 from overseas, a 10-percent return.

In the Pacific Ocean, however, the number of bottles recovered has been consistently smaller. During a seventeen-year period beginning in 1954, scientists from the Scripps Institute cast 148,384 bottles adrift in the Pacific. Only 4,995 were recovered, less than four percent.

"What happened to the other 96.6 percent?" a Scripps scientist asked. He answered his own question: "Our bottles are carefully ballasted with sand to ensure they will float just at the surface. Marine organisms grow on the bottles and they usually sink within eight to ten months unless they are washed ashore earlier. Storms bring many bottles ashore, cast them high on a beach, then bury them in sand. Some are found decades later when wind once more uncovers them.

"The general water movement along the California coast is toward the southeast, toward Baja California. There a few fishing camps manned by Mexican fishermen occupy the long, empty beaches and rocky points. Many bottles find their way ashore on Baja's inhospitable tidelands and, of course, they are lost forever for our use. This cannot help our collection of data."

As for bottles that are never recovered after being dropped into the Atlantic Ocean, Dean F. Bumpus, senior scientist at Woods Hole, answered this way:

"Some become decorations in bars of seaport towns. One bottle was acquired at an auction of a deceased person's effects in Tennessee. It was probably picked up on the coast of Maine, where its mates were found. Some bottles may strand and become buried by wind-blown sand. Some bottles launched off New York were recovered within thirty days near Cape Hatteras. Thirty years later another of the group was found in the same place. It had been buried and later uncovered by a winter storm. Some enter inlets and strand in marshy areas which are seldom frequented except during water-fowl shooting season."

Letters from the Finders

Sometimes, along with the card that reports where a bottle was found, scientists receive letters from people who find bottles. An eighteen-year-old Irish girl named Bridget sent the following note to the U.S. Hydrographic Office:

This bottle was picked up in Clew Bay at a place called the Cathedral Cliffs, Achill Island, County Mayo, Eire, at 11:30 a.m. Tuesday, 9th Sept. I hope the man who deals with this is a fat man. If so, I will surely get a reward. But if it be a thin man, indeed, I have a poor chance, as a fat man is always generous and romantic and I intend to fall in love and marry a fat man.

The Hydrographic Office replied, as it did to all cards, with a letter of thanks, but no reward. The letter also stated where the bottle Bridget found had been launched. Enclosed, too, was a copy of a current chart of the Irish coast.

A young African living in British Somaliland rode a camel across the desert carrying a similar letter and chart that he had received from the Hydrographic Office. His destination: the British consul. Not knowing what the letter said or the chart meant, he hoped he might get a generous reward. He was disappointed when the consul gently informed him that a bank would not cash the chart, no matter how "official" it looked.

Years ago, a young woman found a card in a bottle that promised a reward of fifty cents for returning the card. She sent this letter to Woods Hole:

> I found one of your bottles used for the studying of ocean currents— Everybody says my findings are worth much more—but if 50¢ is all you can afford that's o-kay with me. Please hurry in sending it to me since my parents (cheap skates) give me an allowance so small that I'm continually borrowing from my younger sister. From the reward I will receive only 46¢ since I owe 4¢ to my sister for the stamp.

From Scotland came a letter from a slightly indignant writer a few years ago.

As the enclosed reply card is only for posting in the U.S.A. I am sending you this letter, but no doubt you will refund the postage. The bottle was washed ashore on the Atlantic side of North Uist in the Outer Hebrides. Fifty cents is promised to the sender of the enclosed card, but a small amount of cents is of nae much use here. The Bank will charge 1/— to cash them, and as the bank is sixteen miles fra here, it twa hae to be posted, and they would send the change back in a registered envelope costing a 1/— so there would nae be much left. So I would prefer the equivalent of 50 cents in English currency.

In the spirit of international goodwill, a Woods Hole scientist went to a bank, exchanged a 50-cent piece for four English shillings, and sent the man his reward for finding the card.

Perhaps the strangest letter the Woods Hole scientists ever received was one with a hole in it about the size of a dime. It came with this apologetic note:

My husband couldn't break the bottle—the glass was too thick. So he shot the bottle with his .45 automatic. I guess the bullet went right through your card. Sorry, but maybe you can still use it. Never mind the 50 cents.

Most letters, though, are typical of the one sent to

Texas A&M University by a sixth-grade boy from Bay City, Texas.

Today, Oct. 9, my mother and I were beach combing on the shore of the Gulf of Mexico near the mouth of the Colorado River. We found the enclosed card in a bottle partly sealed with wax. The card was damp but we managed to get it out.

I would like to make a suggestion. It would be interesting to the finder if you put on the card you put in the bottle where and when it was put overboard. Could you please let me know where and when the enclosed card was put overboard?

In his letter, this twelve-year-old boy expressed the thoughts of people everywhere in the world who have ever walked along a beach and found a bottle with a note inside washed onto the sand. Where did it come from? Who sent it? For a moment two souls unknown to each other come into touch in a way made mysterious by the vast sea over which the tiny voyager traveled.

Whether they deliver a note from a scientist seeking knowledge of the restless sea's movements or a desperate appeal from a doomed mariner, seagoing bottles will continue to travel the world's broad oceans. And one might just turn up on anybody's beach.

Index

Albert, Prince of Monaco, 75
Alexander, Daisy, 22

Baldwin, Evelyn, 63–64
Beatty, 31
Bottle messages found in
  Africa, 77, 92
  Australia, 44, 51
  Azores Islands, 11–14
  Bahama Islands, 34
  Canada, 66–67
  England, 37, 53
  Florida 17, 42, 45, 71–72
  France, 57, 77
  Germany, 16
  Hawaii, 51
  Ireland, 37, 46, 91
  Japan, 41
  Maine, 31
  Mexico, 51, 52
  Morocco, 17
  New Guinea, 51
  New Zealand, 78
  North Carolina, 61
  Nova Scotia, 27, 29
  Philippine Islands, 50
  Russia, 63
  San Francisco, 21
  Scotland, 29, 92–93
  Sicily, 43
  South America, 77
  Tasmania, 38

  Texas, 94
  Wales, 39, 78
Bottle messages sent by
  Albert, Prince of Monaco, 75
  Daisy Alexander, 23
  Evelyn Baldwin, 63–64
  Beatty seamen, 31–32
  Benjamin Franklin, 74
  Greek ship captains, 73
  Huronian seamen, 27, 29
  Lusitania passengers, 37
  Chunosuke Matsuyama, 41
  H. Harrison Mayes, 50
  Sir George Nares, 66
  oceanographers, 71–75, 77, 81,
    82–83, 86–87
  passengers on ships, 16
  Robert Peary, 65–66
  Brother George Phillips, 51–52
  Reverend Jewel Pierce, 51
  radio station owner, 13
  seamen, 17, 45
  soldiers, Australian, 38
  spy, English, 55
  Zeppelin L-19, 16
Bottles, seagoing
  drift distance, 78, 79, 80
  drift time, 78, 79, 80
  recovery rate, 88–90
Bottles, tracking with
  currents, 17, 74–75, 80, 81
  fish, 81–82, 87
  jellyfish, 83–84

95

Index

mines, 84
oil, 84, 86
refuse and sewage, 82–83
Bumpus, Dean F., 89–90

Cambria, 34
Carroll A. Deering, 61–62
currents, 74–75, 76, 79, 81–84, 86

Den of Ruthven, 78

Elizabeth, Queen, 54–56

Florida State University, 85
"Flying Dutchman," 79
Franklin, Benjamin, 73–74

Gulf Stream, 74–75, 80

Huronian, 27, 29–30

James, Dr. Wesley P., 86–87

Kent, 33–34

Lennie, 58
Lloyds of London, 28
Loewe, Captain Odo, 16
Lusitania, 35–37

Matsuyama, Chunosuke, 40
Mayes, H. Harrison, 50

Nares, Sir George, 66
National Oceanographic Data
    Center, 85

Oceanographic institutes
    Florida State University, 85
    Scripps Institute of Oceano-
        graphy, 85, 89
    Texas A&M University, 71, 85,
        86, 94

Woods Hole Oceanographic In-
    stitution, 83, 85, 88, 90, 92, 93
Official Uncorker of Ocean Bottles,
    55, 56

Peary, Robert, 65–66
Phillips, Brother George, 51–52
Pierce, Reverend Jewel, 51
President Roosevelt, 16

Roosevelt, 65

Saxilby, 39–40
Schwieger, Kapitän-Leutnant, 35
Scottish Fishery Board, 81
Scripps Institute of Oceanography,
    85, 89
Singer, Isaac, 22
South Carolina Wildlife and Marine
    Resources Department, 87
Strait of Gibraltar, 73
Surface Circulation on the Conti-
    nental Shelf off Eastern North
    America between Newfound-
    land and Florida, 86

Texas A&M University, 71, 85, 86,
    94
Theophrastus, 73
Tirailleur, 58
Tracking with bottles. See Bottles,
    tracking with.

U.S. Department of Commerce, 85
U.S. Navy Hydrographic Office, 80,
    91–92
University of Michigan, 85
U-20, 35, 36

Waratah, 28
Woods Hole Oceanographic Institu-
    tion, 83, 85, 88, 90, 92, 93